SCHOLAST

M000275137

More
Week-by-Week
Sight Word Packets

An Easy System for Teaching 100 Important Sight Words to Set the Stage for Reading Success

Lisa Fitzgerald McKeon

New York · Toronto · London · Auckland · Sydney
New Delhi · Mexico City · Hong Kong · Buenos Aires

Teaching *Resources*

Dedicated to Javier, Luca, and Lola—
without question, the three most important and
cherished words in my vocabulary.

Edited by Mela Ottaiano

Cover design by Lindsey Dekker

Interior design by Melinda Belter

ISBN: 978-0-545-65531-6

Text copyright © 2015 by Lisa Fitzgerald McKeon

Illustrations copyright © 2015 by Scholastic Inc.

Printed in the U.S.A.

2 3 4 5 6 7 8 9 10   40   22 21 20 19 18

Contents

A Note From the Author

For as long as I can remember, the first page of a new book has been full of promise for me. I can recall the excitement I felt as a child each time I walked home from the library, knowing that a newly acquired treasure was safely tucked away in my backpack just waiting to be opened up. It was, in a word, magical. As an adult, things haven't changed much. Books continue to transport me to new places, to new states of mind, and to new experiences. Literacy has been, without a doubt, one of the most powerful tools I have been given in my life.

And so perhaps it is no surprise that I chose literacy as the focus of my adult career. As a Reading Specialist, I assist young children in their acquisition of the deep, well-rooted literacy skills that have served me so well throughout my life. There are, of course, many skills involved in becoming a fluent, accomplished reader. In my professional opinion, one of the first building blocks in this exciting process is to increase a child's sight word vocabulary. The premise is simple—the more words children know, the more able they will be to navigate through a variety of texts and gain meaning from what they have read.

In the pages of this book, I am proud to share the methods and activities I've developed to help young children build up the bank of words they recognize. Time and time again, I've seen children who engage in these activities make great strides in their literacy learning, not only by acquiring the concrete skills they need, but also by developing a love of reading itself. The world of books is indeed a magical one, and I hope this book will help you experience a new kind of magic: the joy that comes from seeing a child discover the endless wonders of the written word.

Enjoy!

Lisa Fitzgerald McKeon

What Are Sight Words and Why Should We Teach Them?

According to educator Robert Hillerich, "Just three words—*I, and, the*—account for ten percent of all words in printed English." Recognizing this, it is easy to see how critical it is that children have a solid grasp of these and other frequently occurring words, for they will be encountering them time and time again in their lives as readers! The activities in this book support young readers by giving them repeated, varied exposure to 100 important sight words. Sight words, also referred to as high-frequency or service words, often cannot be sounded out phonetically. Instead, they need to be recognized "on sight."

Lists of sight words have been around for a long time! In the 1930s after surveying a great quantity of children's books, Edward W. Dolch compiled a list of 220 frequently used words to help parents and educators improve the reading ability of their children. Other commonly used lists include one with 500 words, compiled from the American Heritage Word Frequency Study (Carroll, Davies, and Richman) in the 1970s; and another published by Edward Fry in the 1990s, which incorporates most of the words from the Dolch list, and adds 80 more. This book uses sight words from the American Heritage list. However, all of the lists provide excellent starting points for beginning readers.

As readers acquire a larger bank of sight words, over time they are able to quickly and automatically read these words not only in isolation, but also when encountering them in the context of their reading. This automaticity with words, in turn, leads to even greater gains, because as word recognition skills improve, so does comprehension. Why? Because sounding out each and every word takes up time and brain power. The faster children can recognize words, the more time and energy they'll have to devote to understanding the meaning of the words. Comprehending ideas is, of course, the ultimate goal of reading; and learning sight words is an essential step in reaching that goal.

About This Book

Why *more* sight words? The answer is simple: The more sight words young readers know, the greater their advantage when attempting to read new material. Here is an astonishing fact: Sight words make up over 50 percent of the words in children's texts! The product of my professional research and experience as a reading specialist, *More Week-by-Week Sight Word Packets* follows up on my earlier book, *10 Week-by-Week Sight Word Packets*, by presenting 100 more essential words that readers must recognize on sight. Designed to provide you with a full range of fundamental activities to support early readers, the activities in each unit systematically introduce and reinforce important sight words and have been used successfully with my own students. Each activity is presented in a simple layout that is both easy to understand and fun to complete, promising to engage even the most reluctant readers.

The book is organized into ten units of study that together cover 100 high-frequency sight words. Each unit is a packet of eight pages. The first page introduces ten new sight words, and is followed by seven engaging activity sheets that provide children with repeated multisensory exposure to the targeted sight words. The program is flexible, so you can complete the exercises in order, or pick and choose the particular skills or words you'd like to target (see Instructional Options, page 8).

Equally important, the sheets are designed for quick and easy use— just copy a set and you're ready to go! Because the directions are clear and easy to understand, the activity sheets are ideal for independent work as well as whole-class instruction (see Grouping Options, page 7). And to help students when they are working independently, activities are numbered and ordered on a checklist so they can be checked off when completed. There's also a specific animal icon for each unit and a skill label for each activity.

About the Activity Skills

Each packet is structured to give children repeated practice with new sight words. The skills involved are designed to address four of the key aspects of language development— reading, speaking, writing, and thinking. Finding activities that focus on a particular skill is a snap; just look for the skill label in the top right-hand corner of each activity page. Following are descriptions of each section and skill, plus tips for leading your learners toward mastery.

- **Introducing:** Children are introduced to ten new sight words in each unit. The first page of the unit lets children preview the sounds and spellings they will learn in the upcoming activities. The unit openers also act as a tool for self-monitoring. On the right-hand side of the page, children will see a list of all the activity pages in the unit. Encourage them to check off each activity as they complete it.

- **Tracing:** By tracing and copying, children are focusing on the number of letters within each word, left to right directionality, and the order of the letters. They're also building on letter-sound correspondence.

- **Building:** The repetitive nature of systematically building each sight word, letter by letter, helps reinforce spelling skills.

- **Sorting:** Depending on the font style in a book or the handwriting of an adult, not all sight words look the same to early readers! This activity introduces children to a variety of ways that words can be presented in text.

- **Rewriting:** Being able to recognize the configuration of a sight word is an important skill for developing readers. For example, the words *like* and *look* can present as overly similar to early readers as both words begin with *l* and have a *k*. However, aside from the difference in their meanings, there is also a difference in the physical configuration—or shape—of the words. Early readers need to develop their ability to look at entire words (not just one or two letters) and truly notice such differences.

This rewriting activity provides opportunities for children to attend to how words "look" and begin to ask themselves the important question, "Does that look right?"

- **Searching:** Many children enjoy word searches and what better words to look for than the sight words they have been working on? The words in these searches can be found horizontally ⇨ and vertically ⇩ , which helps reinforce the basic print concept of directionality—left to right, top to bottom.

- **Thinking:** Children comprehend text when they gain meaning from written words. In this activity, children get to see and read in context many of the words they've been practicing, and then show their comprehension by matching each sentence with its corresponding illustration. Each sentence contains one or more of the targeted sight words from that unit.

- **Practicing:** To read fluently, one must be able to speak fluently. This activity gives readers the opportunity to practice reading newly acquired sight words aloud. Children practice reading a word list using a variety of voices with the goal of reading each word automatically, smoothly, and fluently. This activity also invites family members to get involved, reinforcing the crucial school-home connection.

Using the Lessons: Helpful Tips

More Week-by-Week Sight Word Packets is designed for maximum flexibility, so you can easily fit the activities into your curriculum and schedule and tailor them to meet the individual needs of your classroom and students. Following are a few suggestions for making the program a perfect fit for your instructional needs.

Grouping Options

- **Independent Work:** You'll find that the activities in this book are not only lots of fun but also easy for children to understand and complete on their own. You may want to model and review each type of activity throughout the first couple of units; but since the same engaging activity formats are repeated throughout the book, children will likely be able to continue their sight-word learning independently.

- **Partner Work:** Working with a partner can be beneficial for both struggling and advanced readers. When children at different levels work together, the less advanced reader gets support, while the more advanced reader gets the chance to articulate (and therefore reinforce) his or her thinking and problem-solving skills.

- **Small-Group Work:** Working collaboratively helps children gain a variety of skills, as they see how different students approach the same task. Of course, it's also terrific for building social skills!

- **Whole-Class Instruction:** The activities also lend themselves to whole-group instruction. You might consider copying an activity sheet onto chart paper so you can lead the class through the activity as children work with their individual copies. Another option is to scan them to use with an interactive whiteboard.

Instructional Options

- **Complete Program:** You can lead children through the program unit by unit throughout the year, going at a pace that suits your schedule and children's skill level. You may choose to do one unit a week or use another time frame. You may decide to spend more time on some units than on others, or to leave out certain units or activities if you've covered those sight words in another part of your curriculum. There are no hard-and-fast rules—the schedule is all up to you!

- **Target Specific Sight Words:** You may find that children have mastered some sight words, but have trouble achieving automaticity with others. In this case, simply select the activities that cover the specific words children need to practice. Please note that the words in Packet 10 are the longest sight words in this book and may prove particularly tricky for some students.

- **Use as Homework Packets:** You can send the activity sheets home with children to do as independent homework assignments and to foster the school-home connection. Simply send a note home along with the selected activities, explaining what children are learning with the exercises and encouraging parents and caregivers to work with children on the skills they're developing.

Additional Teaching Supports

- **Reproducible Flashcards:** For your convenience and to support student learning, this book includes a complete set of reproducible flashcards for all 100 targeted sight words.

- **Assessment Checklists:** To help you track progress over time and support the instructional needs of all your learners, reproducible Assessment Checklists are provided for all 100 sight words and are conveniently organized by lesson units.

Connections to the Standards

The activities in this book support the College and Career Readiness (CCR) Standards. These broad standards, which serve as the basis of many state standards, were developed to establish grade-by-grade educational expectations meant to provide students nationwide with a quality education that prepares them for college and careers. The activities in each packet correlate with early foundational reading standards for students in grades K–2.

Name _____

Sight Word Packet 1

get

back

go

new

our

through

much

good

write

me

Take a Good Look!

Trace each sight word. Then copy
it on the lines to fill in the glasses.

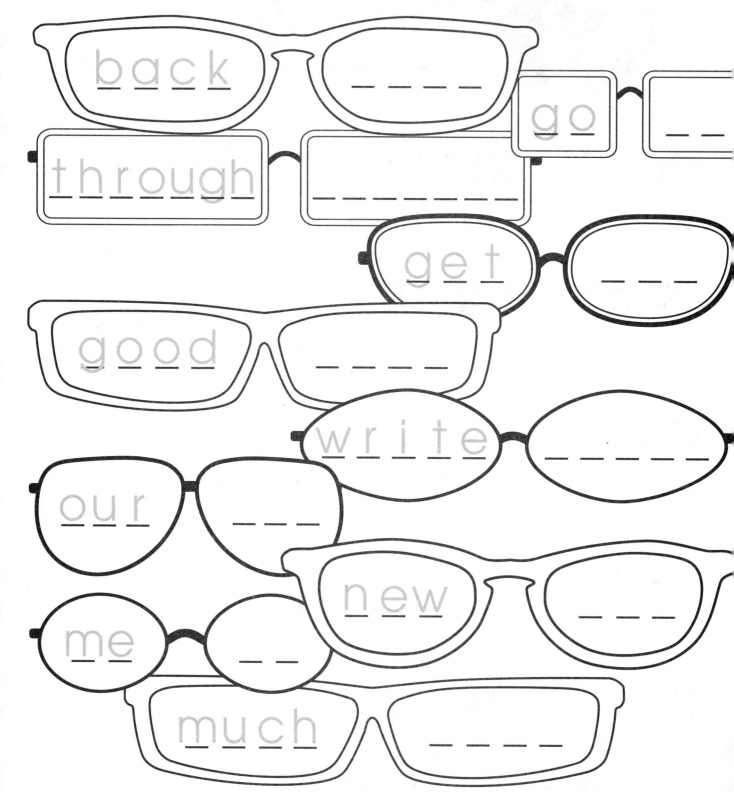

Name _____

One Letter at a Time

Fill in the letters one at a time to build a word pyramid.
One has been done for you.

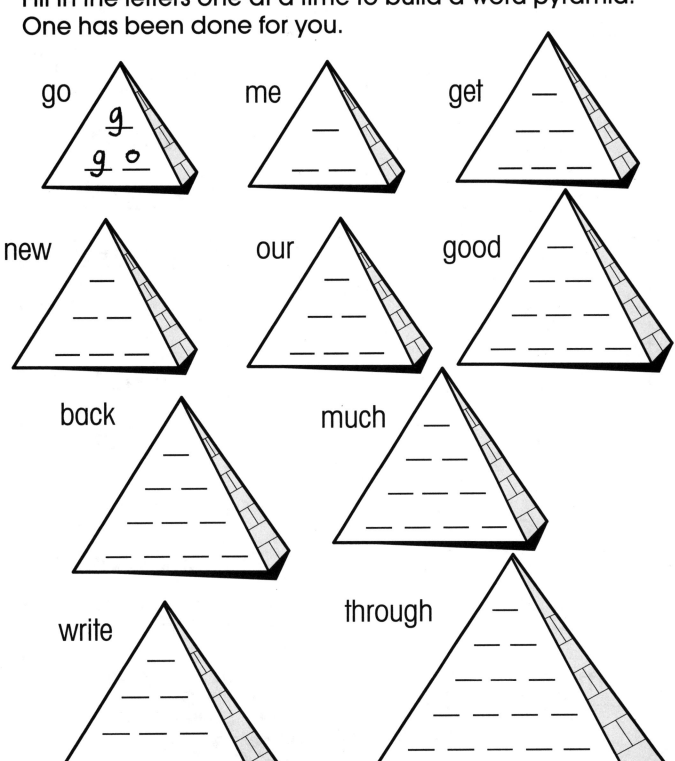

Towering Word Sets

Draw lines from tower to tower to match each set of words.

go

get

new

much

back

write

good

our

me

through

much

back

write

go

get

new

our

through

good

me

Name _____

Get in Shape!

Write each word in the shape box that fits.
One has been done for you.

get   through   our   much   me
good   new   write   back   go

g e t

Name _____

Hide and Seek
Word Search

Use a pencil and circle the words from the list below.
Look for words going across ⇨ and down ⇩ .
One has been done for you.

OUR	THROUGH	BACK	MUCH	GO
~~NEW~~	GOOD	WRITE	GET	ME

```
S  J  Y  G  E  T  M  X  U  B
R  M  E  U  R  H  J  A  R  G
H  H  P  M  W  R  I  T  E  O
I  Y  N  K  X  O  A  X  S  N
S  W  W  A  S  U  E  N  D  R
G  W  I  T  H  G  R  U  I  L
O (N  E  W) B  H  B  L  I  C
O  O  T  H  G  A  M  U  C  H
D  U  H  E  R  S  C  U  B  H
I  R  X  Q  V  Q  B  A  C  K
```

Picture It!

Read each sentence and look at the pictures. Draw a line
to connect each picture with the sentence it goes with.

I will write you a note.

The train can go through
the tunnel.

Can you give the shovel
back to me?

He ate too much cake.

My new dog is a
good boy.

Listen to Me!

Have fun reading each word aloud to your family using the different voices. Be sure to get your paper signed and return it to school.

go

through

back

much

get

new

write

good

me

our

Read these words using a **SCARY** voice.

Read these words using a *silly* voice.

Read these words using a *whisper* voice.

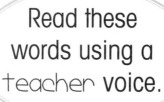

Read these words using a *teacher* voice.

Read these words using a **ROBOT** voice.

_____ read _____ out of 10 words quickly and accurately.

_____ Parent/Guardian Signature

Name _____

Sight Word Packet 2

man

too

any

day

same

right

look

think

also

around

✔ off each activity after you complete it.

❑ Activity 1: **Tracing**

❑ Activity 2: **Building**

❑ Activity 3: **Sorting**

❑ Activity 4: **Rewriting**

❑ Activity 5: **Searching**

❑ Activity 6: **Thinking**

❑ Activity 7: **Practicing**

Name _____

Take a Good Look!

Trace each sight word. Then copy
it on the lines to fill in the glasses.

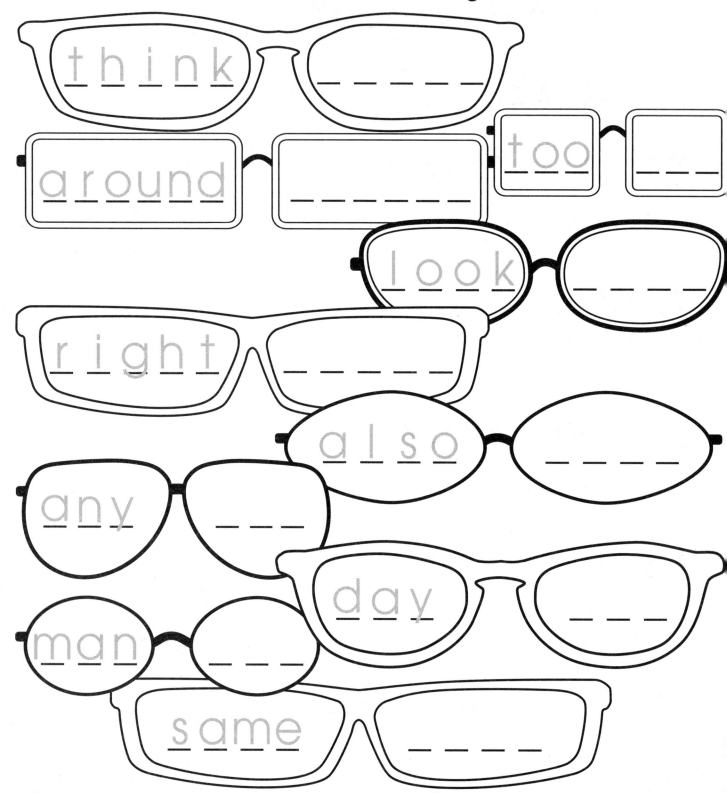

Name _____

One Letter at a Time

Fill in the letters one at a time to build a word pyramid.
One has been done for you.

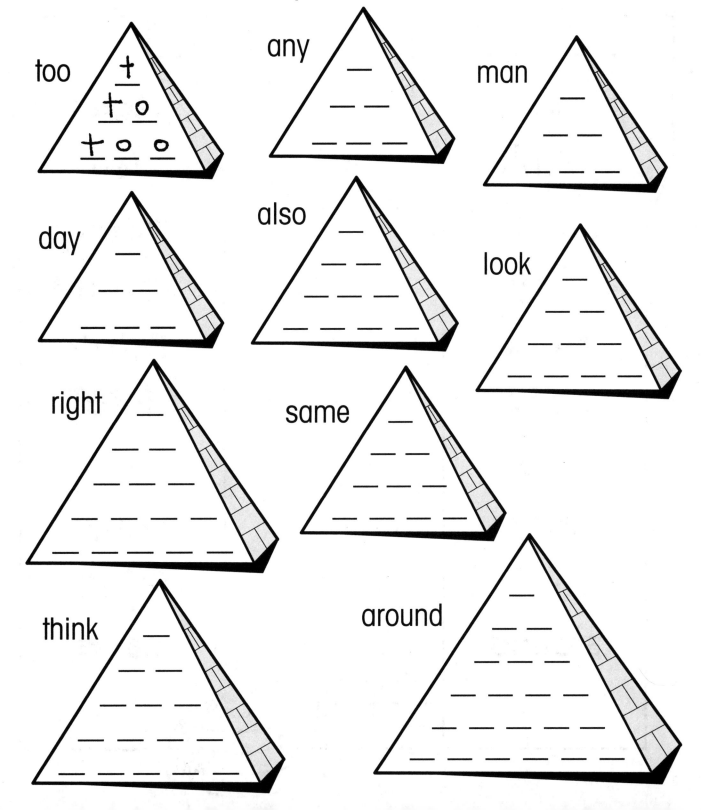

too

any

man

day

also

look

right

same

think

around

Towering Word Sets

Draw lines from tower to tower to match each set of words.

man
think
also
day
same
right
too
any
look
around

right
too
man
around
think
look
any
day
also
same

Name _____

Get in Shape!

Write each word in the shape box that fits.
One has been done for you.

day   man   too   any   same
right   look   think   around   also

| d | a | y |

Name _____

Hide and Seek Word Search

Use a pencil and circle the words from the list below.
Look for words going across ⟹ and down ⬇.
One has been done for you.

| RIGHT | TOO | THINK | DAY | ~~SAME~~ |
| MAN | LOOK | ANY | ALSO | AROUND |

```
A  S  V  L  S  G  U  T  B  A
L  Z  U  C  T  Y  F  W  U  N
G  L  O  O  K  J  Z  F  D  Y
P  U  S  Z (S  A  M  E) W  T
K  H  W  J  V  Q  T  N  D  G
A  R  O  U  N  D  V  R  A  D
L  I  G  C  M  A  N  O  Y  Z
S  G  C  Z  V  H  C  T  Y  A
O  H  T  H  I  N  K  D  S  X
I  T  G  J  N  N  T  O  O  J
```

Name _____

Picture It!

Read each sentence and look at the pictures. Draw a line
to connect each picture with the sentence it goes with.

That man has the same
car as my dad.

Look Mom, I got them
all right!

I think that it is a good
day for ice cream, too.

Can we walk around
the park?

Do you know of any new
books for my son?

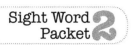

Name _____

Listen to Me!

Have fun reading each word aloud to your family using the different voices. Be sure to get your paper signed and return it to school.

day

too

any

man

same

right

think

look

also

around

Read these words using a **SCARY** voice.

Read these words using a *silly* voice.

Read these words using a *whisper* voice.

Read these words using a *teacher* voice.

Read these words using a **ROBOT** voice.

_____ read _____ out of 10 words quickly and accurately.

_____ Parent/Guardian Signature

Name _____

Sight Word Packet 3

came   come

work   three

must   does

part   even

place   well

Name _____

Take a Good Look!

Trace each sight word. Then copy
it on the lines to fill in the glasses.

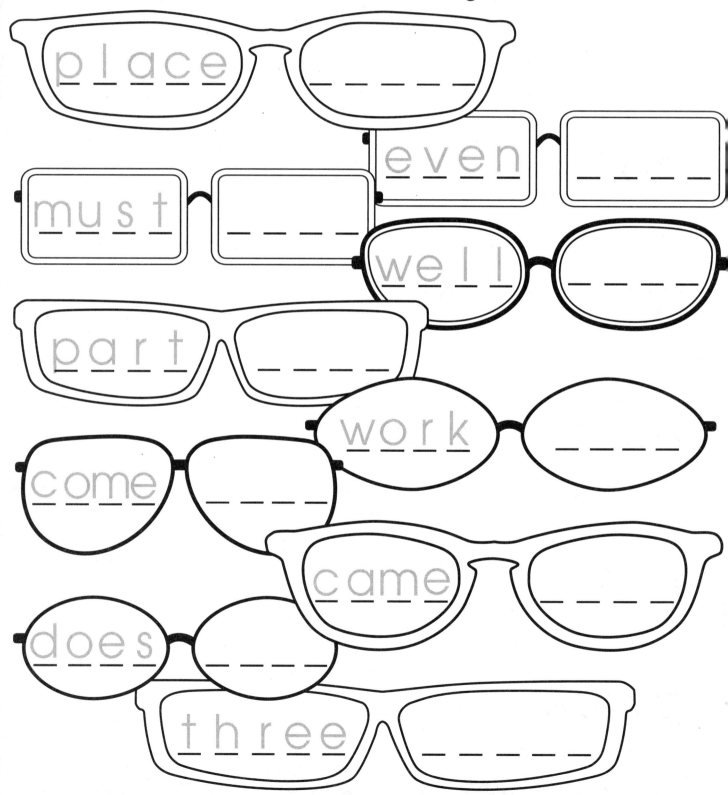

place _____

even _____

must _____

well _____

part _____

work _____

come _____

came _____

does _____

three _____

Name _____

One Letter at a Time

Fill in the letters one at a time to build a word pyramid.
One has been done for you.

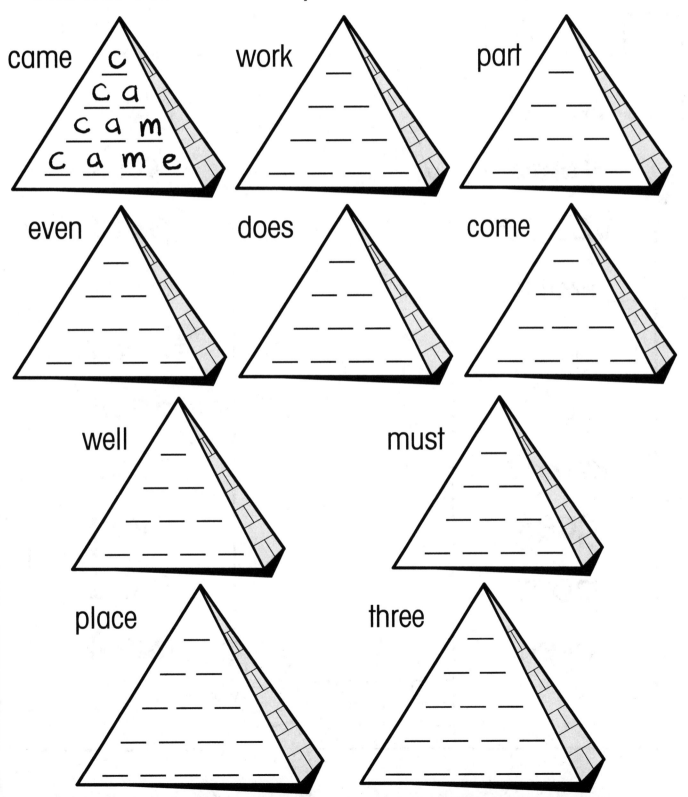

came

c
c a
c a m
c a m e

work

part

even

does

come

well

must

place

three

Towering Word Sets

Draw lines from tower to tower to match each set of words.

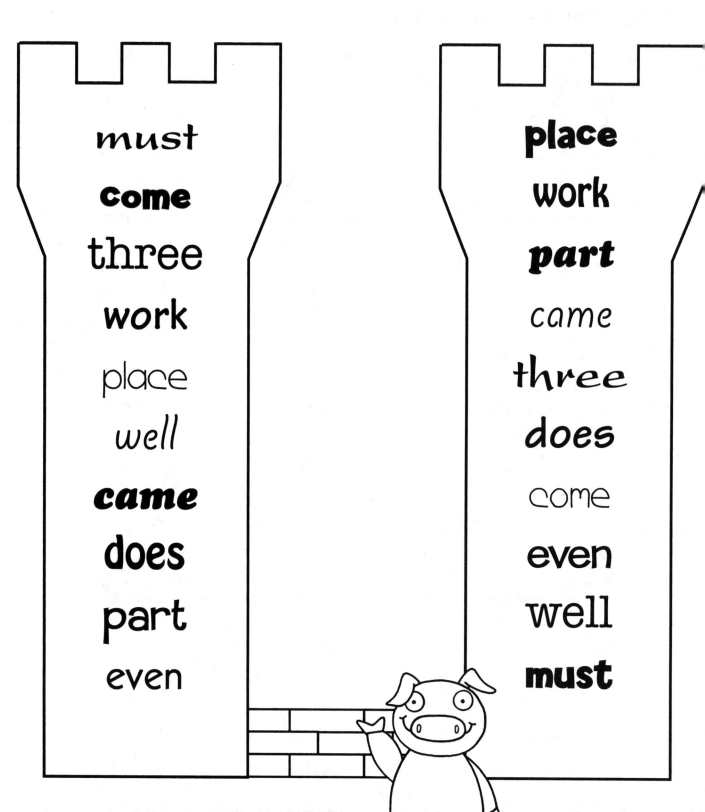

must	**place**
come	work
three	**part**
work	came
place	three
well	does
came	come
does	even
part	well
even	**must**

Name _____

Get in Shape!

Write each word in the shape box that fits.
One has been done for you.

| came | come | ~~work~~ | three | place |
| well | must | does | part | even |

work

Name _____

Hide and Seek Word Search

Use a pencil and circle the words from the list below.
Look for words going across ⇨ and down ⇩.
One has been done for you.

MUST	COME	WORK	PART	PLACE
WELL	CAME	~~DOES~~	THREE	EVEN

```
K  T  T  D  O  E  S  M  X  D
Z  T  A  N  T  W  W  U  P  I
P  J  E  W  F  H  J  S  A  K
L  D  E  B  I  W  H  T  R  B
A  U  T  H  R  E  E  M  T  C
C  J  H  H  X  L  C  E  Q  A
E  V  E  N  S  L  S  V  T  M
J  Z  V  N  P  U  C  A  B  E
W  O  R  K  C  S  P  N  M  M
G  I  C  O  M  E  I  E  V  D
```

Picture It!

Read each sentence and look at the pictures. Draw a line to connect each picture with the sentence it goes with.

My mother goes to work every day.

My brother will come on the ride with me.

She has a big part in the play.

The waiter came over with our drinks.

Three dogs must be three times the work!

Listen to Me!

Have fun reading each word aloud to your family using the different voices. Be sure to get your paper signed and return it to school.

part

even

work

three

place

well

must

does

come

came

Read these words using a SCARY voice.

Read these words using a silly voice.

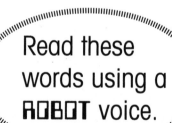

Read these words using a whisper voice.

Read these words using a teacher voice.

Read these words using a ROBOT voice.

_____ read _____ out of 10 words quickly and accurately.

_____ Parent/Guardian Signature

Name _____

Sight Word Packet 4

such   here

take   why

help   put

away   again

off   went

✔ off each activity after
you complete it.

❑ Activity 1: **Tracing**

❑ Activity 2: **Building**

❑ Activity 3: **Sorting**

❑ Activity 4: **Rewriting**

❑ Activity 5: **Searching**

❑ Activity 6: **Thinking**

❑ Activity 7: **Practicing**

Name _____

Take a Good Look!

Trace each sight word. Then copy
it on the lines to fill in the glasses.

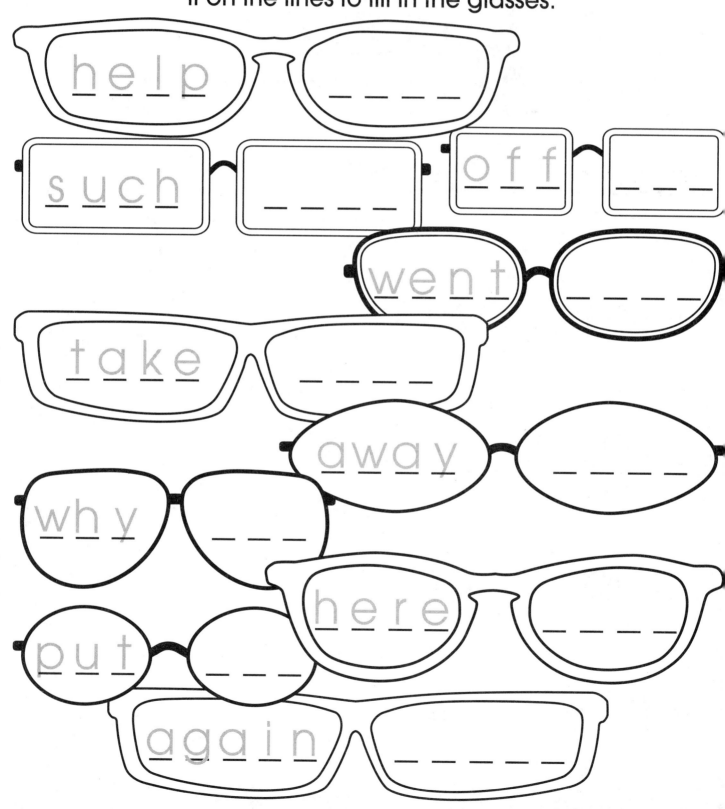

help _____

such _____

off _____

went _____

take _____

away _____

why _____

here _____

put _____

again _____

Name _____

One Letter at a Time

Fill in the letters one at a time to build a word pyramid.
One has been done for you.

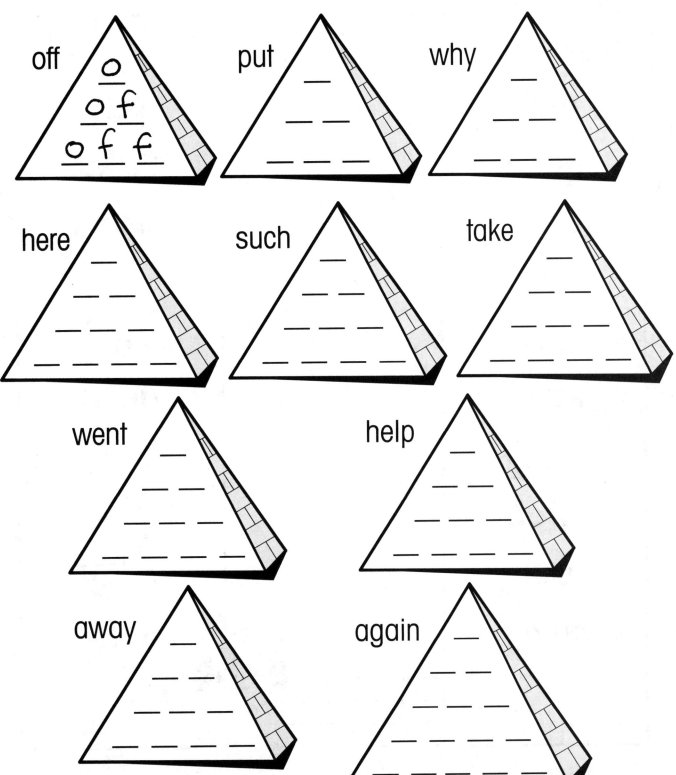

Towering Word Sets

Draw lines from tower to tower to match each set of words.

help

here

take

again

off

went

why

such

put

away

put

take

away

such

off

here

went

again

why

help

Name _____

Get in Shape!

Write each word in the shape box that fits.
One has been done for you.

| such | here | take | again | off |
| went | ~~why~~ | help | put | away |

w h y

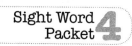

Hide and Seek Word Search

Use a pencil and circle the words from the list below.
Look for words going across ⇨ and down ⬇.
One has been done for you.

| HERE | SUCH | TAKE | AGAIN | OFF |
| WHY | WENT | HELP | ~~PUT~~ | AWAY |

```
Q W G A H W T J C S
W E Y J E O F F N U
H N L S R L E Y Y C
Y T A K E L A G Y H
X D G F F E R E N T
H B A F S M U U P R
B L I C L A Z T U S
T Q N T S J P B T B
H E L P T Z K E C I
V I M D A W A Y U M
```

Picture It!

Read each sentence and look at the pictures. Draw a line to connect each picture with the sentence it goes with.

I put on boots when it snows.

I help my dad do the dishes.

Why are you crying again?

Here is my truck.

The thief tried to take my balloon away.

Listen to Me!

Have fun reading each word aloud to your family using the different voices. Be sure to get your paper signed and return it to school.

again

here

take

such

put

went

why

help

off

away

Read these words using a **SCARY** voice.

Read these words using a *silly* voice.

Read these words using a *whisper* voice.

Read these words using a *teacher* voice.

Read these words using a **ROBOT** voice.

_____ read _____ out of 10 words quickly and accurately.

_____ Parent/Guardian Signature

Name _____

Sight Word Packet 5

old

tell

say

every

still

great

men

small

found

name

✔ off each activity after you complete it.

❑ Activity 1: **Tracing**

❑ Activity 2: **Building**

❑ Activity 3: **Sorting**

❑ Activity 4: **Rewriting**

❑ Activity 5: **Searching**

❑ Activity 6: **Thinking**

❑ Activity 7: **Practicing**

Name _____

Take a Good Look!

Trace each sight word. Then copy
it on the lines to fill in the glasses.

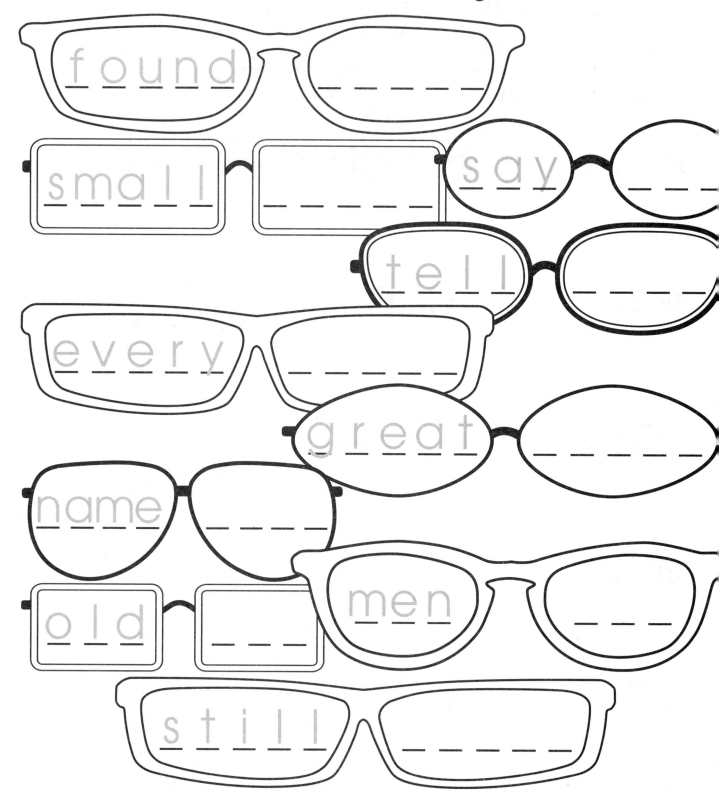

found _____

small _____

say ___

tell _____

every _____

great _____

name _____

old ___

men ___

still _____

One Letter at a Time

Fill in the letters one at a time to build a word pyramid.
One has been done for you.

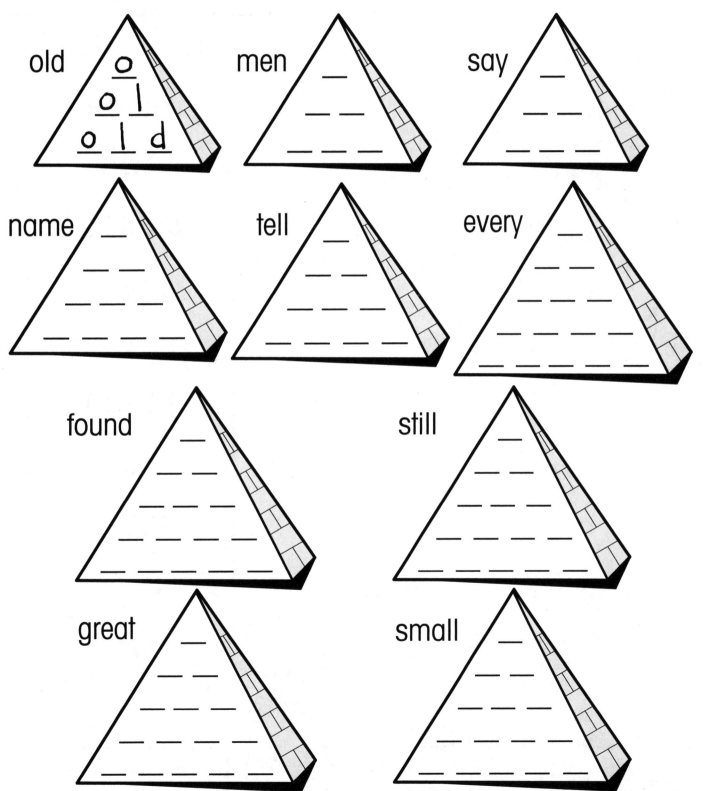

old

o
o l
o l d

men

say

name

tell

every

found

still

great

small

Name _____

Towering Word Sets

Draw lines from tower to tower to match each set of words.

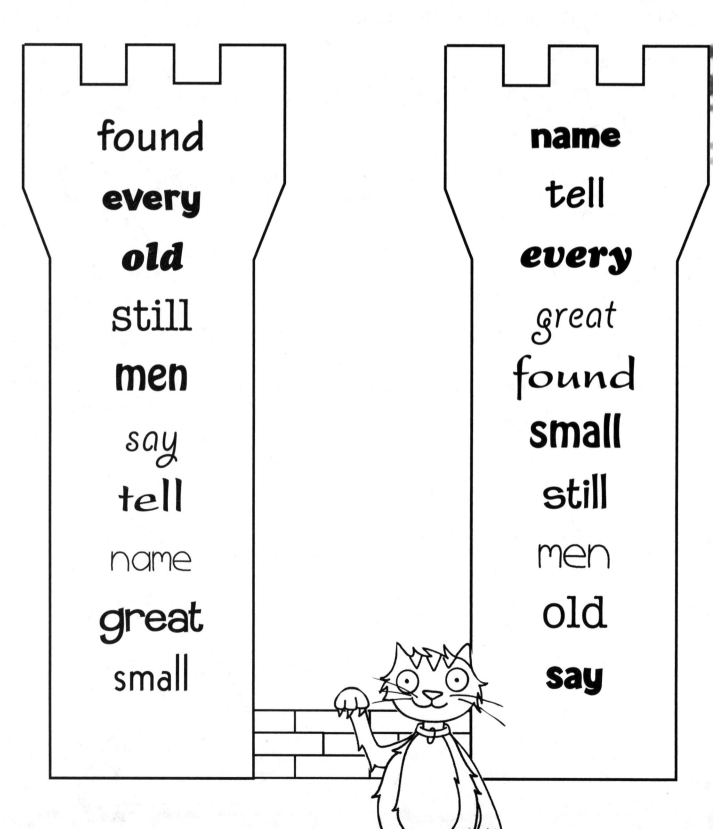

found	**name**
every	tell
old	**every**
still	great
men	found
say	**small**
tell	still
name	men
great	old
small	**say**

Name _____

Get in Shape!

Write each word in the shape box that fits.
One has been done for you.

| old | every | found | still | name |
| great | ~~tell~~ | men | say | small |

t e l l

Hide and Seek Word Search

Use a pencil and circle the words from the list below.
Look for words going across ⇨ and down ⬇.
One has been done for you.

OLD	EVERY	SAY	STILL	NAME
~~GREAT~~	TELL	MEN	FOUND	SMALL

```
X S A A U S M A L L
D T G L R T L X W N
O I A G M V M E N A
E L I N I L G A W M
O L F O U N D R E E
S D L Y I S S A N T
A X E O M G M B T C
Y D L O L D A D O G
E V E R Y L T E L L
X G R E A T L T A X
```

Name _____

Picture It!

Read each sentence and look at the pictures. Draw a line to connect each picture with the sentence it goes with.

The men are taking a walk.

I am three years old!

What did you say?

The boy found a small bug.

Hi! My name is Anna.

Listen to Me!

Have fun reading each word aloud to your family using the different voices. Be sure to get your paper signed and return it to school.

say

small

found

still

name

great

tell

men

old

every

Read these words using a **SCARY** voice.

Read these words using a silly voice.

Read these words using a whisper voice.

Read these words using a teacher voice.

Read these words using a **ROBOT** voice.

_____ read _____ out of 10 words quickly and accurately.

_____ Parent/Guardian Signature

Name _____

Sight Word Packet 6

should   home

big   give

air   line

set   own

under   read

Name _____

Take a Good Look!

Trace each sight word. Then copy
it on the lines to fill in the glasses.

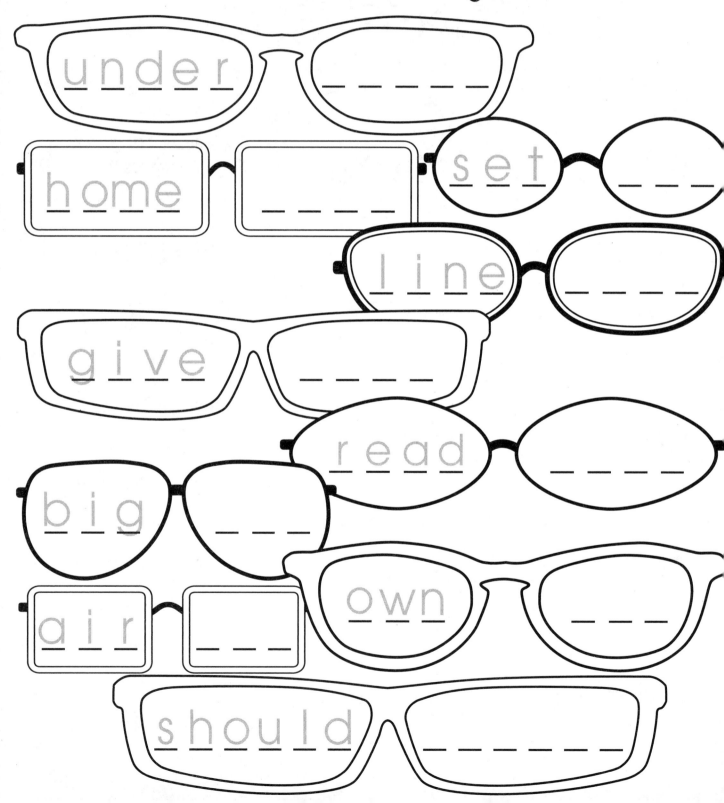

One Letter at a Time

Fill in the letters one at a time to build a word pyramid.
One has been done for you.

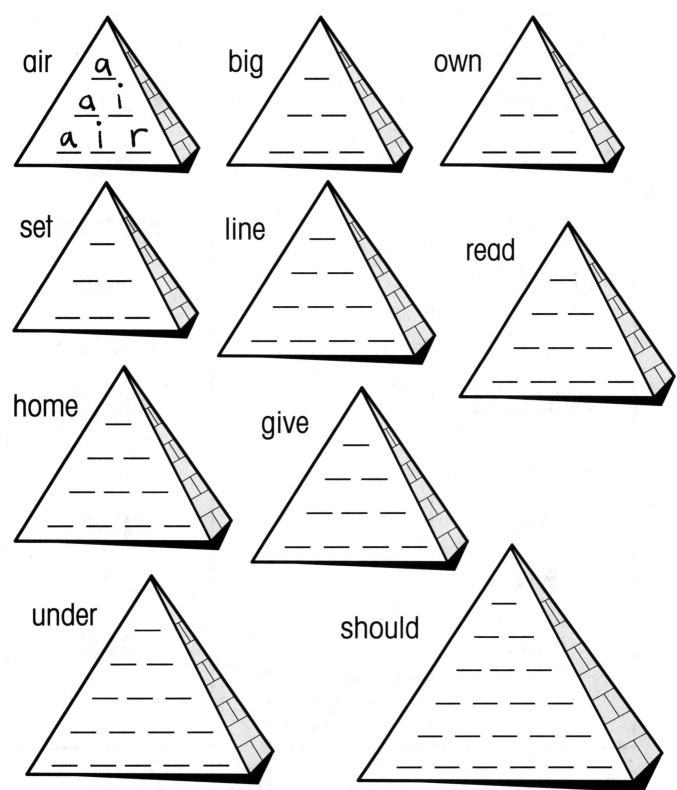

air

a
a i
a i r

big

own

set

line

read

home

give

under

should

Towering Word Sets

Draw lines from tower to tower to match each set of words.

line
set
own
under
give
should
home
air
big
read

should
big
home
own
under
read
line
give
air
set

Get in Shape!

Write each word in the shape box that fits.
One has been done for you.

Activity 4

Rewriting

| line | ~~set~~ | own | under | read |
| should | home | big | give | air |

s | e | t

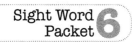

Hide and Seek Word Search

Use a pencil and circle the words from the list below.
Look for words going across ⇨ and down ⇩.
One has been done for you.

HOME	SET	OWN	AIR	READ
SHOULD	LINE	B̶I̶G̶	GIVE	UNDER

```
E  T  R  A  I  R  V  E  R  Y
J  G  G  Y  H  E  K  I  W  K
F  S  L  I  N  E  L  B  I  G
O  E  Q  R  I  G  K  S  O  I
M  T  P  E  H  P  A  H  P  V
O  W  N  A  G  Y  H  O  M  E
D  E  G  D  A  W  E  U  H  V
T  E  I  A  O  P  R  L  P  I
C  N  S  A  M  P  C  D  H  V
L  T  U  N  D  E  R  Q  F  N
```

Name _____

Picture It!

Read each sentence and look at the pictures. Draw a line to connect each picture with the sentence it goes with.

We read lots of great books.

You should share your toys.

We own a big home.

The plane flew through the air.

I like to sit under the apple tree.

Name _____

Listen to Me!

Have fun reading each word aloud to your family using the different voices. Be sure to get your paper signed and return it to school.

air

set

own

under

read

should

home

big

give

line

Read these words using a **SCARY** voice.

Read these words using a silly voice.

Read these words using a *whisper* voice.

Read these words using a teacher voice.

Read these words using a **ROBOT** voice.

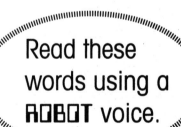

_____ read _____ out of 10 words quickly and accurately.

_____ Parent/Guardian Signature

Name _____

Sight Word Packet 7

last

never

us

left

end

along

while

might

next

sound

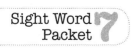

Take a Good Look!

Trace each sight word. Then copy
it on the lines to fill in the glasses.

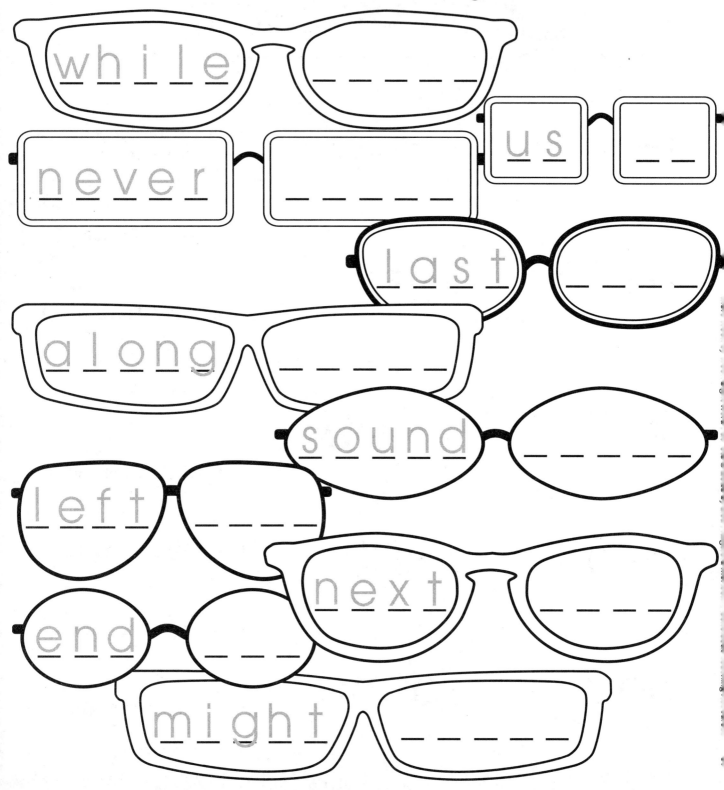

while _____

never _____

us __

last _____

along _____

sound _____

left _____

next _____

end _____

might _____

Name _____

One Letter at a Time

Fill in the letters one at a time to build a word pyramid.
One has been done for you.

us
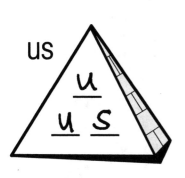
u
u s

end
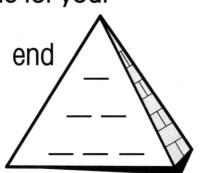

next
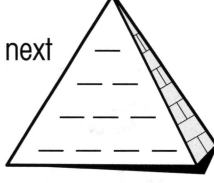

last
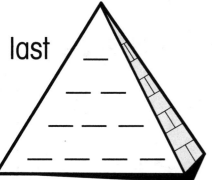

never
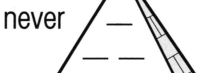

left
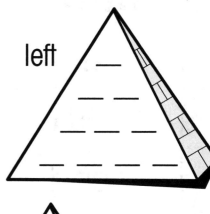

along
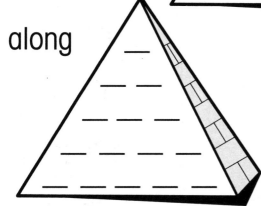

while
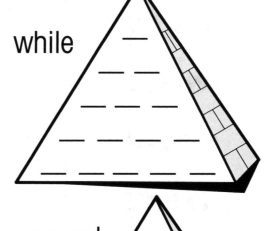

might

sound

Name _____

Sorting

Towering Word Sets

Draw lines from tower to tower to match each set of words.

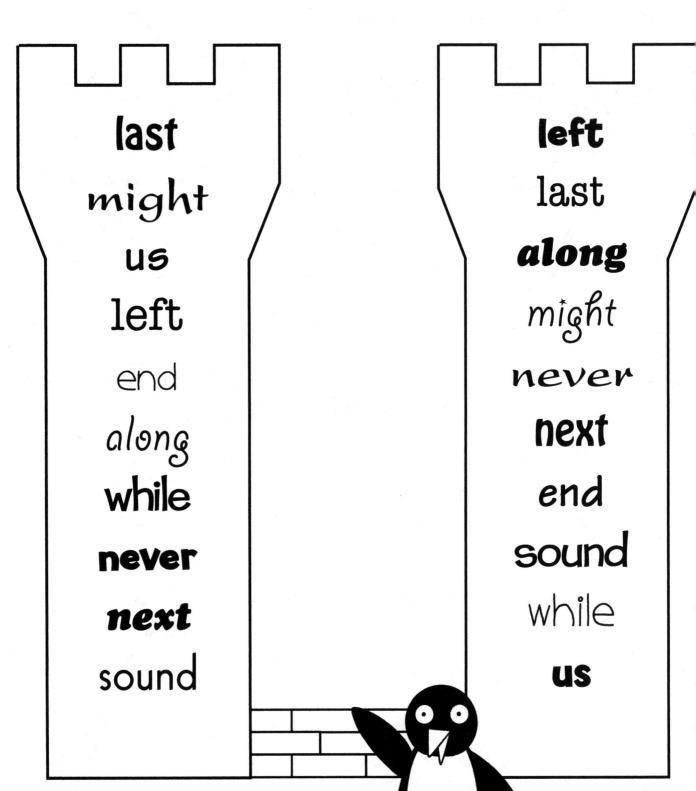

last	left
might	last
us	along
left	might
end	never
along	next
while	end
never	sound
next	while
sound	us

Name _____

Get in Shape!

Write each word in the shape box that fits.
One has been done for you.

along	while	might	next	sound
~~last~~	never	us	left	end

l a s t

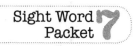

Hide and Seek Word Search

Use a pencil and circle the words from the list below.
Look for words going across ⇨ and down ⬇.
One has been done for you.

ALONG	WHILE	LAST	NEXT	SOUND
MIGHT	NEVER	US	LEFT	~~END~~

```
M  L  G  N  E  V  E  R  T  G
G  A  L  E  S  T  B  K  B  E
L  S  O  X  F  N  A  A  E  O
E  T  X  T  O  U  G  V  N  U
N  L  A  D  U  N  O  W  N  L
D  Q  R  A  S  D  K  H  F  E
A  D  A  L  R  E  A  I  N  F
T  M  S  O  U  N  D  L  X  T
M  I  G  H  T  S  A  E  Q  C
H  J  T  A  L  O  N  G  V  Q
```

Picture It!

Read each sentence and look at the pictures. Draw a line to connect each picture with the sentence it goes with.

There's only one leaf left on the tree.

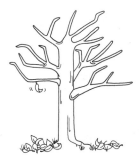

The last two cookies are for us.

A tuba can make a really big sound.

She had a bow at the end of her braid.

He drove the car along the road.

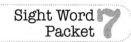
Listen to Me!

Have fun reading each word aloud to your family using the different voices. Be sure to get your paper signed and return it to school.

never

while

last

next

sound

might

along

us

left

end

Read these words using a **SCARY** voice.

Read these words using a *silly* voice.

Read these words using a *whisper* voice.

Read these words using a *teacher* voice.

Read these words using a **ROBOT** voice.

_____ read _____ out of 10 words quickly and accurately.

_____ Parent/Guardian Signature

Name _____

Sight Word Packet 8

below

both

those

show

often

saw

few

always

large

asked

✔ off each activity after
you complete it.

❏ Activity 1: **Tracing**

❏ Activity 2: **Building**

❏ Activity 3: **Sorting**

❏ Activity 4: **Rewriting**

❏ Activity 5: **Searching**

❏ Activity 6: **Thinking**

❏ Activity 7: **Practicing**

Name _____

Take a Good Look!

Trace each sight word. Then copy
it on the lines to fill in the glasses.

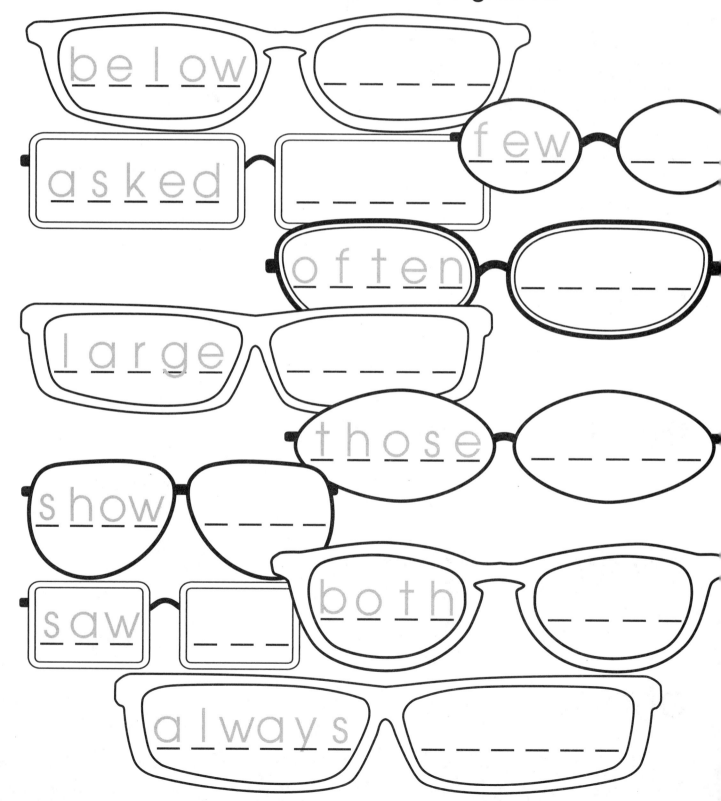

below _____

asked _____ few ___

often _____

large _____ those _____

show _____

saw ___ both _____

always _____

Name _____

One Letter at a Time

Fill in the letters one at a time to build a word pyramid.
One has been done for you.

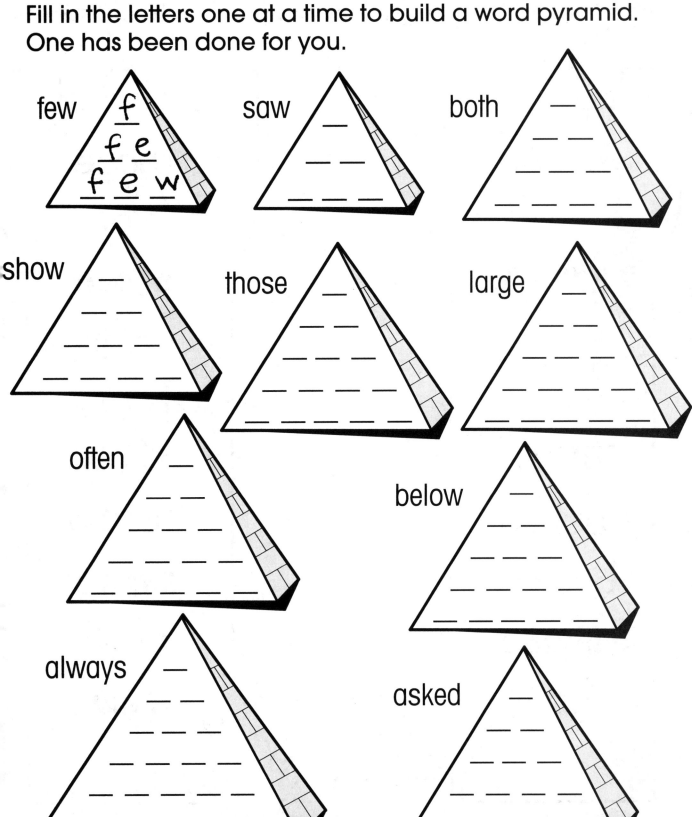

few

saw

both

show

those

large

often

below

always

asked

Name _____

Towering Word Sets

Draw lines from tower to tower to match each set of words.

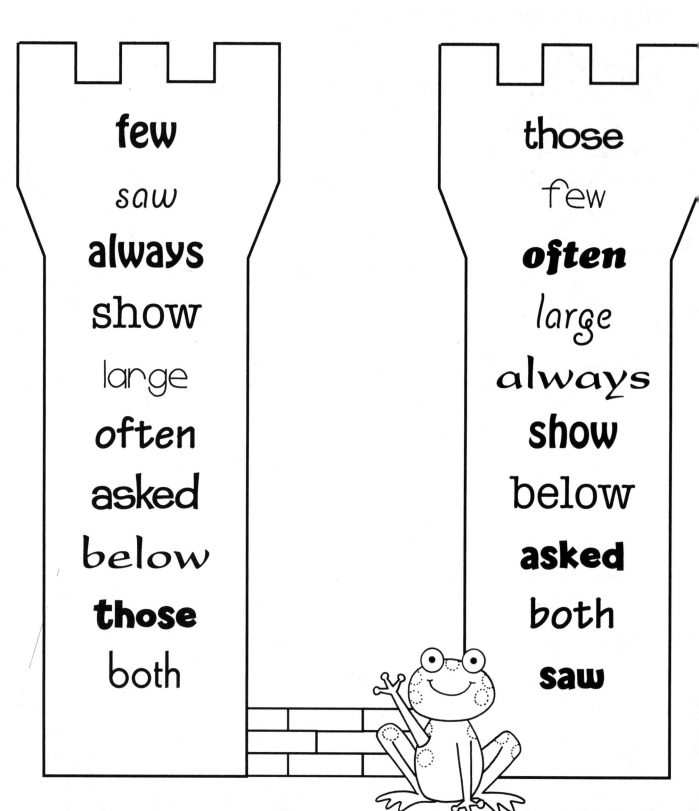

few	**those**
saw	few
always	**often**
show	large
large	always
often	**show**
asked	below
below	**asked**
those	both
both	**saw**

Name _____

Get in Shape!

Write each word in the shape box that fits.
One has been done for you.

few   those   always   show   large

often   asked   below   saw   ~~both~~

b o t h

Hide and Seek Word Search

Use a pencil and circle the words from the list below.
Look for words going across ⇨ and down ⬇ .
One has been done for you.

ALWAYS	THOSE	LARGE	SHOW	FEW
OFTEN	ASKED	BELOW	~~SAW~~	BOTH

```
R  D  B  N  Y  I  J  F  E  W
A  S  K  E  D  H  O  S  R  I
V  O  A  L  W  A  Y  S  M  N
M  P  Y  A  H  I  T  E  I  E
Q  V  A  R  K  S  H  O  W  X
L  X  J  G  H  O  O  G  H  T
G  I  O  E  R  F  S  L  T  B
B  E  L  O  W  T  E  R  X  O
S  A  W  Q  X  E  M  T  C  T
V  T  B  K  R  N  W  F  E  H
```

Name _____

Picture It!

Read each sentence and look at the pictures. Draw a line to connect each picture with the sentence it goes with.

I often get a large ice cream cone.

She asked me to show her the way.

We saw a few ducks on the pond.

The carrots are on the shelf below the milk.

They both play baseball.

Name _____

Listen to Me!

Have fun reading each word aloud to your family using the different voices. Be sure to get your paper signed and return it to school.

saw

both

always

show

large

often

asked

below

few

those

Read these words using a **SCARY** voice.

Read these words using a silly voice.

Read these words using a whisper **voice**.

Read these words using a teacher **voice**.

Read these words using a **ROBOT** voice.

_____ read _____ out of 10 words quickly and accurately.

_____ Parent/Guardian Signature

Name _____

Sight Word Packet 9

house   don't

world   going

want   school

until   form

food   keep

Name _____

Take a Good Look!

Trace each sight word. Then copy
it on the lines to fill in the glasses.

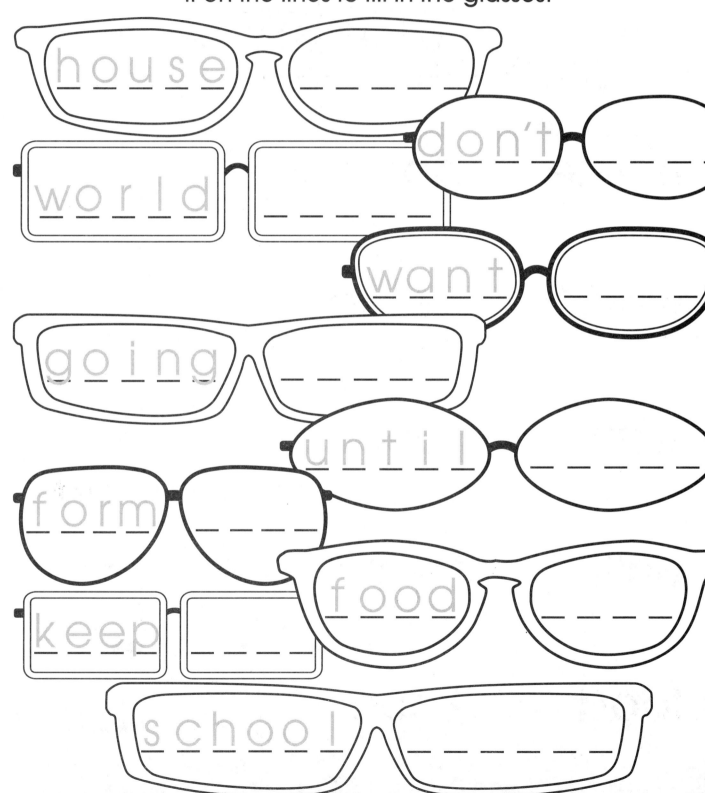

house _____

don't _____

world _____

want _____

going _____

until _____

form _____

food _____

keep _____

school _____

Name _____

One Letter at a Time

Fill in the letters one at a time to build a word pyramid.
One has been done for you.

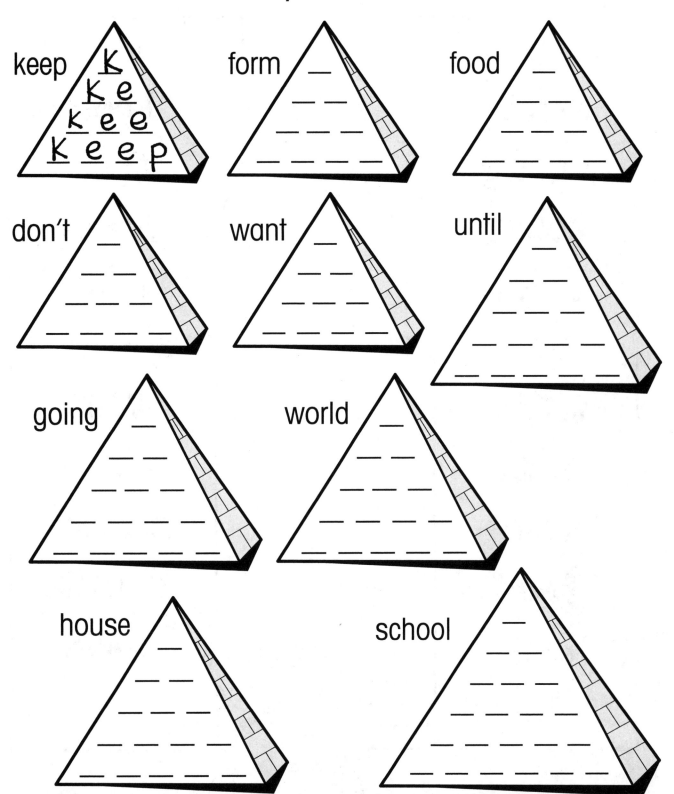

keep

k
k e
k e e
k e e p

form ___

food ___

don't ___

want ___

until ___

going ___

world ___

house ___

school ___

Towering Word Sets

Draw lines from tower to tower to match each set of words.

world	keep
going	food
house	form
don't	until
want	going
school	want
until	house
form	school
food	don't
keep	world

Name _____

Get in Shape!

Write each word in the shape box that fits.
One has been done for you.

school   don't   form   going   want
house   until   world   ~~food~~   keep

f o o d

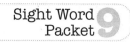

Activity
Searchin

Hide and Seek Word Search

Use a pencil and circle the words from the list below.
Look for words going across ⇨ and down ⇩.
One has been done for you.

FOOD	~~DON'T~~	WORLD	GOING	KEEP
SCHOOL	UNTIL	FORM	HOUSE	WANT

```
K  E  E  P  W  E  G  Y  H  V
A  F  O  O  D  P  H  M  O  S
G  H  Z  T  P  F  I  S  U  B
O  A  Y  U  F  T  P  C  S  A
I  W  A  N  T  E  T  H  E  R
N  T  X  T  X  N  D  O  N  T
G  F  K  I  X  Z  R  L  X  E
A  E  S  L  L  W  O  R  L  D
V  W  R  E  K  F  O  R  M  E
S  C  H  O  O  L  J  R  F  O
```

Name _____

Picture It!

Read each sentence and look at the pictures. Draw a line to connect each picture with the sentence it goes with.

There's a pond near our house.

We keep our dog's food in a big bowl.

I don't want to eat it!

The world is an amazing place.

We like going to school.

Listen to Me!

Have fun reading each word aloud to your family using the different voices. Be sure to get your paper signed and return it to school.

form

food

keep

going

want

school

until

house

don't

world

Read these words using a **SCARY** voice.

Read these words using a silly voice.

Read these words using a whisper voice.

Read these words using a teacher **voice.**

Read these words using a **ROBOT** voice.

_____ read _____ out of 10 words quickly and accurately.

_____ Parent/Guardian Signature

Name _____

Sight Word Packet 10

another

because

different

number

between

something

thought

together

important

children

✔ off each activity after you complete it.

❏ Activity 1: **Tracing**

❏ Activity 2: **Building**

❏ Activity 3: **Sorting**

❏ Activity 4: **Rewriting**

❏ Activity 5: **Searching**

❏ Activity 6: **Thinking**

❏ Activity 7: **Practicing**

Take a Good Look!

Trace each sight word. Then copy
it on the lines to fill in the glasses.

something _ _ _ _ _ _ _ _ _

different _ _ _ _ _ _ _ _ _

important _ _ _ _ _ _ _ _ _

together _ _ _ _ _ _ _ _

children _ _ _ _ _ _ _ _

One Letter at a Time

Fill in the letters one at a time to build a word pyramid.

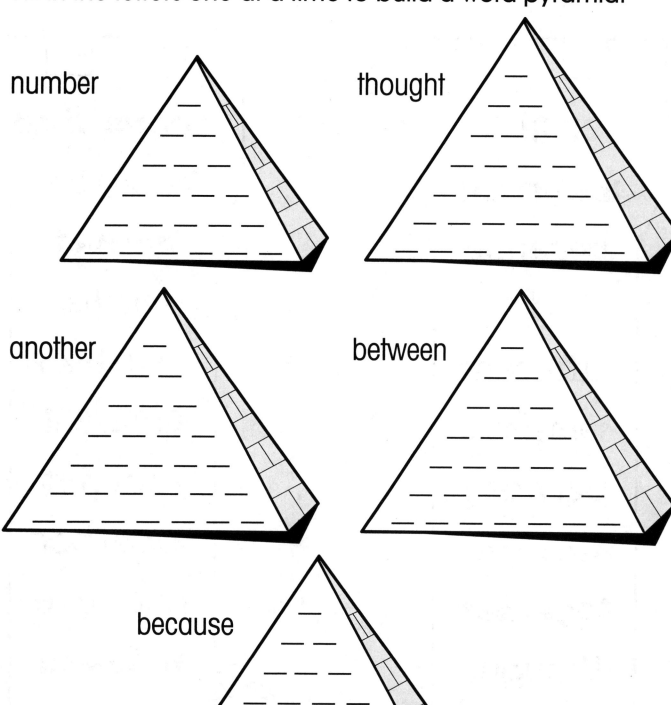

number

thought

another

between

because

Towering Word Sets

Draw lines from tower to tower to match each set of words.

another
important
because
children
different
something
between
number
together
thought

something
important
number
another
children
different
thought
together
because
between

Get in Shape!

Write each word in the shape box that fits.

thought   children   because

another   number   between   together

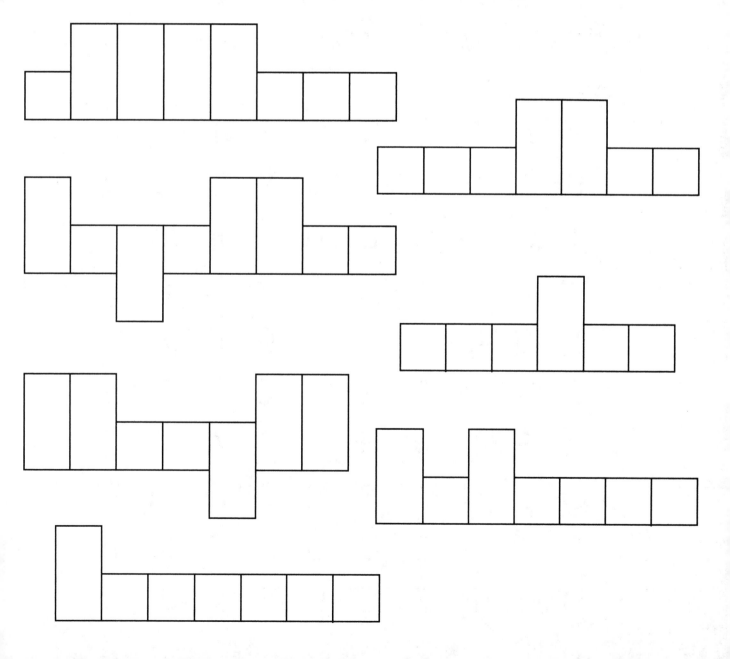

Hide and Seek Word Search

Use a pencil and circle the words from the list below.
Look for words going across ⇨ and down ⬇ .
One has been done for you.

ANOTHER	IMPORTANT	NUMBER	~~CHILDREN~~	BETWEEN
SOMETHING	THOUGHT	BECAUSE	TOGETHER	DIFFERENT

```
B  E  C  A  U  S  E  I  S  W
E  F  H  N  S  O  N  M  O  D
T  G  I  O  E  M  U  P  M  T
W  E  L  T  N  E  M  O  E  O
E  U  D  H  O  T  B  R  F  G
E  M  R  E  G  H  E  T  R  E
N  B  E  R  H  I  R  A  I  T
O  E  N  I  E  N  Z  N  M  H
S  T  H  O  U  G  H  T  G  E
D  I  F  F  E  R  E  N  T  R
```

Picture It!

Read each sentence and look at the pictures. Draw a line to connect each picture with the sentence it goes with.

I thought of something wonderful today.

He has a scrape because he fell down.

The children are doing different things at the playground.

It is important to eat healthy foods.

I was sitting between Mom and Dad.

Listen to Me!

Have fun reading each word aloud to your family using the different voices. Be sure to get your paper signed and return it to school.

between

important

because

children

different

something

thought

number

together

another

Read these words using a **SCARY** voice.

Read these words using a silly voice.

Read these words using a *whisper* voice.

Read these words using a *teacher* voice.

Read these words using a **ROBOT** voice.

_____ read _____ out of 10 words quickly and accurately.

_____ Parent/Guardian Signature

too

day

right

think

around

man

any

same

look

also

through

much

good

write

me

get

back

go

new

our

here	such	come	came
Sight Word Packet 4	Sight Word Packet 4	Sight Word Packet 3	Sight Word Packet 3
why	take	three	work
Sight Word Packet 4	Sight Word Packet 4	Sight Word Packet 3	Sight Word Packet 3
put	help	does	must
Sight Word Packet 4	Sight Word Packet 4	Sight Word Packet 3	Sight Word Packet 3
again	away	even	part
Sight Word Packet 4	Sight Word Packet 4	Sight Word Packet 3	Sight Word Packet 3
went	off	well	place

old	great		should	home
tell	men		big	give
say	small		air	line
every	found		set	own
still	name		under	read

saw	below	last
Sight Word Packet 8		Sight Word Packet 7
few	both	never
Sight Word Packet 8		Sight Word Packet 7
always	those	left
Sight Word Packet 8		Sight Word Packet 7
large	show	along
Sight Word Packet 8		Sight Word Packet 7
asked	often	end
		Sight Word Packet 7
		while
		Sight Word Packet 7
		might
		Sight Word Packet 7
		sound
		next

because	Sight Word Packet 10
another	Sight Word Packet 10
number	Sight Word Packet 10
different	Sight Word Packet 10
something	Sight Word Packet 10
between	Sight Word Packet 10
together	Sight Word Packet 10
thought	Sight Word Packet 10
children	Sight Word Packet 10
important	Sight Word Packet 10
don't	Sight Word Packet 9
house	Sight Word Packet 9
going	Sight Word Packet 9
world	Sight Word Packet 9
school	Sight Word Packet 9
want	Sight Word Packet 9
form	Sight Word Packet 9
until	Sight Word Packet 9
keep	Sight Word Packet 9
food	Sight Word Packet 9

Sight Words Reading Assessment: 100 More

Student Name _____

UNIT 1				UNIT 2				UNIT 3				UNIT 4				UNIT 5		
Assessment Dates				Assessment Dates				Assessment Dates				Assessment Dates				Assessment Dates		
1	2	3		1	2	3		1	2	3		1	2	3		1	2	3
			get				man				came				such				old
			through				too				come				here				great
			back				any				work				take				tell
			much				day				three				why				men
			go				same				must				help				say
			good				right				does				put				small
			new				look				part				away				every
			write				think				even				again				found
			our				also				place				off				still
			me				around				well				went				name

Student Name _____

UNIT 6	UNIT 7	UNIT 8	UNIT 9	UNIT 10
Assessment Dates	Assessment Dates	Assessment Dates	Assessment Dates	Assessment Dates

UNIT 6 — 1 2 3

- should
- home
- big
- give
- air
- line
- set
- own
- under
- read

totals

UNIT 7 — 1 2 3

- last
- never
- us
- left
- end
- along
- while
- might
- next
- sound

totals

UNIT 8 — 1 2 3

- below
- saw
- both
- few
- those
- always
- show
- large
- often
- asked

totals

UNIT 9 — 1 2 3

- house
- don't
- world
- going
- want
- school
- until
- form
- food
- keep

totals

UNIT 10 — 1 2 3

- another
- because
- different
- number
- between
- something
- thought
- together
- important
- children

totals

Answers

Sight Word Packet 1

```
S J Y G E T M X U B
R M E U R H J A R G
H H P M W R I T E O
I Y N K X O A X S N
S W W A S U E N D R
G W I T H G R U I L
O N E W B H B L I C
O O T H G A M U C H
D U H E R S C U B H
I R X Q V Q B A C K
```

Sight Word Packet 2

```
A S V L S G U T B A
L Z U C T Y F W U N
G L O O K J Z F D Y
P U S Z S A M E W T
K H W J V Q T N D G
A R O U N D V R A D
L I G C M A N O Y Z
S G C Z V H C T Y A
O H T H I N K D S X
I T G J N N T O O J
```

Sight Word Packet 3

```
K T T D O E S M X D
Z T A N T W W U P I
P J E W F H J S A K
L D E B I W H T R B
A U T H R E E M T C
C J H H X L C E Q A
E V E N S L S V T M
J Z V N P U C A B E
W O R K C S P N M M
G I C O M E I E V D
```

Sight Word Packet 4

```
Q W G A H W T J C S
W E Y J E O F F N U
H N L S R L E Y Y C
Y T A K E L A G Y H
X D G F F E R E N T
H B A F S M U U P R
B L I C L A Z T U S
T Q N T S J P B T B
H E L P T Z K E C I
V I M D A W A Y U M
```

Sight Word Packet 5

```
X S A A U S M A L L
D T G L R T L X W N
O I A G M V M E N A
E L I N I L G A W M
O L F O U N D R E E
S D L Y I S S A N T
A X E O M G M B T C
Y D L O L D A D O G
E V E R Y L T E L L
X G R E A T L T A X
```

Sight Word Packet 6

```
E T R A I R V E R Y
J G G Y H E K I W K
F S L I N E L B I G
O E Q R I G K S O I
M T P E H P A H P V
O W N A G Y H O M E
D E G D A W E U H V
T E I A O P R L P I
C N S A M P C D H V
L T U N D E R Q F N
```

Sight Word Packet 7

```
M L G N E V E R T G
G A L E S T B K B E
L S O X F N A A E O
E T X T O U G V N U
N L A D U N O W N L
D Q R A S D K H F E
A D A L R E A I N F
T M S O U N D L X T
M I G H T S A E Q C
H J T A L O N G V Q
```

Sight Word Packet 8

```
R D B N Y I J F E W
A S K E D H O S R I
V O A L W A Y S M N
M P Y A H I T E I E
Q V A R K S H O W X
L X J G H O O G H T
G I O E R F S L T B
B E L O W T E R X O
S A W Q X E M T C T
V T B K R N W F E H
```

Sight Word Packet 9

```
K E E P W E G Y H V
A F O O D P H M O S
G H Z T P F I S U B
O A Y U F T P C S A
I W A N T E T H E R
N T X T X N D O N T
G F K I X Z R L X E
A E S L L W O R L D
V W R E K F O R M E
S C H O O L J R F O
```

Sight Word Packet 10

```
B E C A U S E I S W
E F H N S O N M O D
T G I O E M U P M T
W E L T N E M O E O
E U D H O T B R G G
E M R E G H E T R E
N B E R H I R A T T
O E N I E N Z N M H
S T H O U G H T G E
D I F F E R E N T R
```